Beautiful

Bracelets

for beginners
and beyond

Contents

Over 40 Bracelets

Brick & Ladder Stitch

Herringbone Stitch

Needle Weaving

Peyote Stitch

Right Angle Weave

Spiral Rope

Square Stitch

Wire Knitting

Special thanks to our designers

Erika Barna
Di Noyce
Mary Mott
Beverley Wells
and to
Jo Gardner *for gallery pictures*
Jenny Knight *for inspiring bead mixes*
Lynda Pederson of Olaf Beadwork
and **The Beaders Network**
who taught me to square stitch.

EDITOR: Jill Oxton

DISTRIBUTION ENQUIRIES

Jill Oxton Publications Pty Ltd
PO Box 283
Park Holme,
South Australia 5043

PH within Aust: (08) 8276 2722

PH outside Aust: 61 8 8276 2722

FAX: (08) 8374 3494

EMAIL: jill@jilloxtonxstitch.com

Beautiful Bracelets
for beginners and beyond

ISBN 0-9587576-3-1

PHOTOGRAPHY BY BARDON

REPROGRAPHICS BY GRAPHIC PRINT GROUP

PRINTED IN CHINA BY BOOKBUILDERS

THE HARDEST THING TO
DO WHEN STITCHING THESE
BRACELETS, IS DECIDING
WHAT COLOURS TO USE.

Bracelets are an ideal way to practise a new stitch. While working the first one, you can get a feel for the stitch and think about different colour, style, and bead combinations.

A bracelet strip can be adapted to many uses, such as earrings, rings, hair clips,watch straps, chokers, edgings for book covers, spectacle chains, serviette rings, belts, animal collars and dress straps.

Between projects and when you don't know what to do, make a bracelet. They make ideal presents .... if you can bear to part with them.

Smaller beads make a more delicate looking bracelet than larger beads as shown in our examples left and right, of similar style bracelets.

The dainty bracelet on page 4 was worked using 11/0 Delica's with 4mm diameter round beads.

The chunky bracelet on the right was worked in 4mm squares and 6mm diameter round beads.

We hope you get as many hours of pleasure in making these bracelets as we did.

Best wishes,

Basic Tools & Equipment

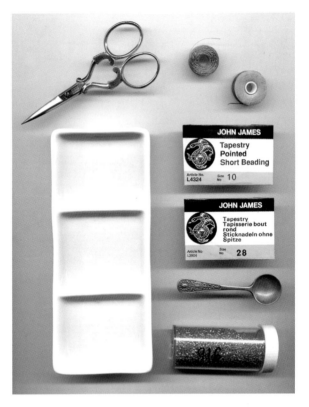

SCISSORS: I use an old pair of embroidery scissors as quite often they are used to cut fine-gauge wire.

THE THREAD: I prefer Nymo D which is a very strong, but fine, multi-filament nylon thread available in a wide variety of colours. It works particularly well with a blunt beading needle.

Pre-stretch your Nymo thread by pulling it inch by inch through your fingers and stretching it at the same time. This is particularly useful for removing the curls from the thread when you are getting to the end of a bobbin and could also help if you have a very loose tension.

I have also found that Black Nymo D tends to be thicker than some other colours. You will need to keep this in mind if you are doing a lot of weaving back and forth or if your beads have small holes.

Match your thread to the main colour of your beads and bear in mind that if you are using transparent beads, the thread will affect their colour. This can be an advantage as well as a disadvantage.

Cut your thread as long as you can manage it (around 2 metres). You will find there is an optimum working length for you, this is when you achieve the minimum amount of twists and tangles. I cut my thread about twice the length of my outstretched arm and find this a workable length.

THE NEEDLE: I use a John James No. 10 Tapestry Pointed Short Beading Needle. Delica's will also accept a John James 28 Tapestry Needle, easier to thread, but they do break easily.

Avoid forcing a needle through a bead as you may break it, instead change to a finer needle or discard the bead. If the needle is tight the first time through the bead discard it as it could break when working subsequent rows.

If you have trouble threading your needles, remember that a needle's eye has a right and wrong side to it. Try rotating the needle so the reverse side of the eye is facing you and this should prove much easier.

BEAD SPOON: As beads bounce, I use an antique salt spoon to remove the beads from their container. You could use a plastic spoon, but I do think if you use beautiful things it makes you feel more beautiful.

BEAD CONTAINERS: To store my beads, I use clear plastic vials with screw top lids (*not pop top or your beads will go everywhere*) purchased from an outlet that distributes vials to chemists (or buy them from your local chemist). Using a permanent felt tip pen, I mark the bead colour on the side of the container and on the lid. Being clear, these vials can be placed on their side in a drawer and you can see at a glance the colours. A cheaper alternative are plastic zip lock bags.

BEAD DISH: The small and inexpensive ceramic condiment dish pictured on page 6 works perfectly for me. It has sloped sides and is heavy so is not easily dislodged. I use these to hold my beads when stitching.

Do not use plastic trays, you will spend more time picking up your beads than you will beading.

BEADING BOARD: You can purchase one or use a tray with side edges on it. It should be large enough to hold your pattern and bead tray(s).

BEADING MAT: A hemmed corduroy square between 20cm to 30cm (8" to 12") square is very useful, particularly when unpicking, as the beads do not bounce on it. Some beaders I know like to place their beads on it instead of using containers such as a ceramic dish.

SMALL NEEDLE-NOSE OR CHAIN-NOSE PLIERS: Used to attach jewellery findings to your bracelets. If your needle does get stuck in your beading, pull it through with a small pair of needle-nose pliers. After a little experience you can judge whether the bead will break or not. Unfortunately you will have to break a few beads to gain this experience.

Pliers are also useful if you made a mistake you didn't pick up and it really needs correcting. Place needle inside offending bead *(to avoid cutting thread)*, crush the bead with pliers and insert the correct bead. This will not be perfect as thread from the crushed bead will show.

Made a mistake earlier in your beading which you haven't picked up?

The American Indians call this a spirit bead and believe it is meant to be there.

The Japanese, call this a humility bead.

The Amish and Moslems deliberately keep a mistake in their work, as they believe the only thing that is perfect is God.

I believe in all of the above and then, just hope to do better next time.

NAIL VARNISH: Used to seal knots on findings, so they will not unravel and to stiffen beading. You will find that the nail varnish will harden further after several hours, so if desired the beading can be moulded into a shape while touch dry and before it hardens.

We use Sally Hansen Double Duty Clear Top Coat.

OTHER USEFUL ITEMS

A METAL BOARD with magnetic strips such as those produced by LoRan are ideal for holding your chart and keeping your place.

ROUND NOSE PLIERS: These have cone shaped tips useful for wirework. *It is also easier to use two pair of pliers when opening a jump ring.*

DIAGONAL WIRE CUTTERS: For cutting wire.

DO'S & DON'TS

WHEN UNPICKING: Always unthread your needle as you can get into a real tangle if you run your needle back through the beads.

DON'T CHANGE THE TYPE/SIZE OF THREAD you use within a piece as this can affect the tension and cause distortion of the beading.

ALWAYS use a new thread when attaching findings *(see page 11 & 104).*

GLUES: Don't use super-glue on your beads, it doesn't work and can affect the finish. E6000 is a tested glue to use with beading. Imported from the USA, it is strong, clear and dries quickly. Always test your beads by placing some into a drop of glue to see if there are any adverse reactions between the bead and the glue before using any glues.

AVOID ANODISED BEADS as the colour can wear off. You can seal them but I would rather steer clear of them, particularly for bracelets which do take a lot of wear and tear. *Our example below right shows what happened with anodised beads after a period of wear.*

Bead Information

How Many Beads
An approximate guide

	Per Gram	Per CM
11/0 Japanese Cylinder Beads ...... *Delica/Magnifica/Toho* *You will get around 500 beads in a 3 gram packet.*	165	7
15/0 Seed Beads	290	9
11/0 Seed Beads	110	7
8/0 Seed Beads	38	5
6/0 Seed Beads	15	4
Small Bugle Beads *(6mm)*	43	
Medium Bugle Beads *(9mm)*........	27	
Large Bugle Beads *(14mm)*	13	

Using Bugle Beads

 *Versus*

To obtain the best results when using bugle beads, it is very important to sort them first.

Discard any bugles with broken ends as they could cut your thread and sort into the same length and width.

Sort them in height by placing them between two magnet strips or rules on your work board and lay the bugles out side by side.

Sort them in width by eye. After working with beads for a little while, you soon get very attuned to the difference in sizes.

I realise that this is fiddly and time consuming (*it took me about an hour to sort out the bugles for the gold bracelet),* but as you will be spending several hours making the bracelet it is well worth the effort.

When stitching with bugles, try to place a seed bead at either end, of the bugle. This will help to stop the edges of the bugle cutting your thread.

Sizing Your Bracelet

The average size of a bracelet is around 18cm complete with findings.

1 Measure your wrist and add about .5cm ($^3/_8''$) - depending on the style of bracelet.

2 Deduct assembled length of the findings, *(cover tips, jump rings and clasps)* that will be attached to the bracelet. *These can vary from around 1.5cm to 3cm ($^5/_8''$ to $1^1/_4''$).*

3 Make the beaded section of the bracelet this length.

Wrist plus .5cm ($^3/_8''$)
- less findings
= length of beaded strip.

Findings

See pages 101 to 104.

We cannot stress too much how important it is to use a new piece of thread to attach your findings.

The toggle for the RAW slinky bracelet shown on page 51 does not go through the ring. By using a new piece of thread it is so much easier to cut the finding off and replace it, or use more beads on the loop so the toggle can twist enough to fit through the ring.

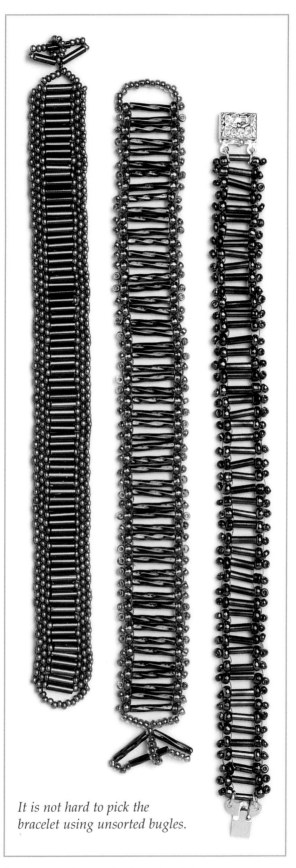

It is not hard to pick the bracelet using unsorted bugles.

Brick & Ladder Stitch

Brick Stitch (also known as Commanche Stitch) is a very useful stitch, easy to work with no reflection line. It looks like Peyote Stitch turned on its side, can be used with a Peyote Stitch chart and is in fact easier to work when a lot of increasing and decreasing is involved on shaped items.

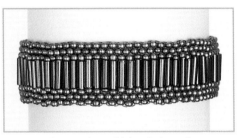

Above: The gold bugle bracelet was worked using brick stitch.

Above: The blue bugle bracelet was worked using ladder stitch.

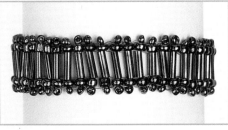

Above: The blue bugle bracelet was worked using ladder stitch. and the bugles were not sorted to the same height.

LADDER STITCH

Use Ladder Stitch to make straps or as a foundation for brick stitch. Our diagram doesn't show it, but you can stitch through each bead twice to strengthen the ladder. Keep tension firm, but not tight or you will find it difficult to catch up the thread when working the second row.

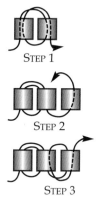

STEP 1
STEP 2
STEP 3

STEP 1: Pick up two beads and sew together working clockwise.

STEP 2: Pick up one bead and attach by sewing anti clockwise.

STEP 3: Pick up one bead and attach by sewing clockwise.

Continue working anti clockwise and clockwise until the ladder is the desired length.

BRICK STITCH

Diagram 1 (below): The top row shows the foundation row of ladder stitch. The second row is brick stitch.

At the beginning of every row always pick up two beads.

Pass the needle behind and then over the loop and back down through the bead the thread is exiting, so that the bead is hanging on a thread loop.

Continue by picking up one bead at a time, making one stitch per loop and pulling thread taut.

Brick Stitch can be worked from right to left, or left to right.

DIAGRAM 1

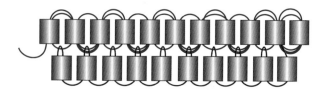

BRICK STITCH INCREASE ON THE OUTSIDE EDGE

An increase on the outer edge is made by working Ladder Stitch to the desired length (Diagram 2).

Ladder stitch can be worked from left to right, or right to left.

DIAGRAM 2

BRICK STITCH DECREASE ON THE OUTSIDE EDGE

Weave thread back through beads to the correct position and commence the row with two beads (Diagram 3).

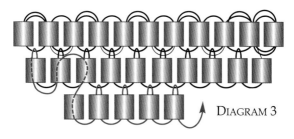

DIAGRAM 3

STARTING & FINISHING THREADS IN BRICK STITCH

Weave thread ends in and out of at least five beads and then diagonally through another five beads. Pull taut and cut thread.

To start a thread, take thread through about five beads, pull end into bead and then weave in and out of at least five beads to sewing position.

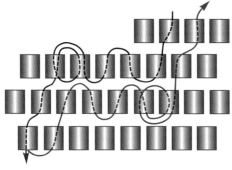

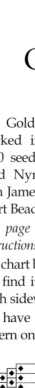

Gold Bugle

BY JILL OXTON

The Gold Bugle Bracelet was worked in brick stitch using 11/0 seed beads, bugle beads, Gold Nymo D thread and a John James 10 Tapestry Pointed Short Beading Needle.

See page 14 for brick stitch instructions.

The chart below has been turned as I find it easier to work brick stitch sideways.

We have also written out the pattern on the next page.

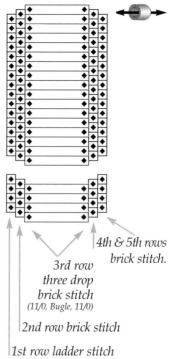

4th & 5th rows brick stitch.

3rd row three drop brick stitch (11/0, Bugle, 11/0)

2nd row brick stitch

1st row ladder stitch

REQUIREMENTS FOR A
16 CM LENGTH

83 x 6mm high Bugles
550 x 11/0 Seed Beads
Nymo D thread.

The Pattern

Cut thread about 2 metres (80") long.

Row 1: Ladder stitch using 11/0 seed beads for the length of the bracelet, less 1cm ($^3/_8$") - *more if you are not using our clasp.*

Remember that the first stitch for a brick stitch row is actually two stitches.

Row 2: Coming out of the **first** bead *(you may need to turn your ladder)*, brick stitch using 11/0 seed beads. Increase at the end by working one ladder stitch.

Row 3: *Three drop brick stitch* - Coming out of the **first** bead, start by picking up 1 seed, 1 bugle, 2 seed, 1 bugle, 1 seed and work the first two stitches; and then for the remainder of the stitches for this row, pick up 1 seed, 1 bugle, 1 seed. Increase at the end by working one three drop ladder stitch.

Row 4: Coming out of the **second** *three drop,* brick stitch using 11/0 seed beads.

Row 5: Coming out of the **second** bead, brick stitch using 11/0 seed beads and weave thread ends into beading securely.

The Closure

The Loop: Using a new thread, come out of the second row on the side edge of the bracelet, thread up 11 x 11/0 seed beads and go into row 4.

To strengthen the clasp, weave to other side edge of bracelet and through loop once more, then finish off.

The Toggle: Using a new thread, come out of the second row on the other side edge of the bracelet, thread up 8 x 11/0 seed beads and go into row 4.

Weave to other side of bracelet and through the first four beads of the loop once more.

Pick up 1 bugle, 4 x 11/0 seed beads, 1 bugle, 4 x 11/0 seed beads, 1 bugle and run thread through the second half of the loop.

Weave to other side of bracelet and through the first four beads of the loop once more and pick up 9 x 11/0 seed beads and wrap these around the centre of the toggle. Weave back through second half of loop and finish off thread ends.

Blue Bugle

BY JILL OXTON

The Blue Bugle Bracelet was worked in ladder stitch using 11/0 and 8/0 seed beads, 7mm high bugle beads, Blue Nymo D thread and a John James 10 Short Blunt Beading Needle.

See page 14 for ladder stitch instructions.

REQUIREMENTS FOR A 16 CM LENGTH

52 x *6mm or 9mm high* Bugles
104 x 11/0 Seed Beads
104 x 8/0 Seed Beads
Nymo D thread.
1 x 2 hole Clasp
4 x 5mm Jump Rings

The Pattern

Cut thread about 2 metres (80″) long.

STEP 1: Using 8/0 seed beads, ladder stitch (*going through each bead twice*) for the length of the bracelet (*less size of clasp when assembled*) and put aside.

STEP 2: Make another ladder using the same amount of beads as used in step 1. Turn this ladder so the thread is exiting on the top left side.

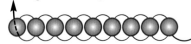

STEP 3 - CENTRE: Pick up 1 x bugle and go through first bead of the second ladder Diag 2, finishing row in this manner.

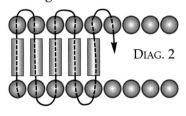

DIAG. 2

The two hole clasp above was attached to the bracelet using jump rings

STEP 4 - *The top and bottom edge is worked using 11/0 seed beads which lie on their sides:*

DIAGRAM 3 - Coming out of the top of the first 8/0 bead, **pick up 1 x 11/0**, and go down *8/0, bugle, 8/0.*

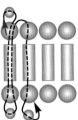

Pick up 1 x 11/0 and go back up through *bottom 8/0, bugle and top 8/0.* Go down through *8/0, bugle, 8/0* in the next row and **pick up 1 x 11/0.**

DIAGRAM 4 - Go up through *8/0, bugle and 8/0.* **Pick up 1 x 11/0** and go back down through *8/0, bugle, 8/0.* Then go through *8/0, bugle and 8/0* of the next row and **pick up 1 x 11/0.**

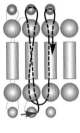

DIAGRAM 5 - Go down through *8/0, bugle, 8/0.* **Pick up 1 x 11/0** and go back up *8/0, bugle, 8/0.*

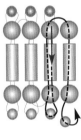

Go down the beads of the next row and **pick up 1 x 11/0.**

Continue in this manner for the length of the bracelet and weave in thread ends.

SEE PAGE 17 FOR CLASP DETAILS
Note that the number of beads strung may need to be adjusted for larger bugles.

Herringbone Stitch

Herringbone Stitch *(also known as Ndebele Weave)* can be used for the same sort of charted designs as square stitch and is worked using pairs of beads. We have shown the simplest form of Herringbone stitch here.

Above: Herringbone with 3mm squares.

Above: Herringbone with 11/0 Delica's and 15/0 seed beads, slipped on.

Above: Tubular Herringbone

HERRINGBONE STITCH

ALSO KNOWN AS NDEBELE WEAVE

Different stitches need a different tension and it can take a while to work out the correct tension for a stitch.

Using Delica 11/0's - DBR42 and 15/0 Japanese Seed Beads in black and gold, I worked some swatches in herringbone stitch, starting with a ladder stitch base.

These are suitable for bracelets or straps and gave me an idea of what works with herringbone stitch.

I found that in a straight piece (with no increases) a firm, but not tight tension worked best for me. See examples below. Now that I have the tension worked out, *and if I remember*, with a little more practise I am sure my weave will get better.

1   Worked in 11/0 Delica's as diagrams 1 to 4 right.

2   11/0 Delica's with a 15/0 slipped between each pair of herringbone on Row 4 and then every 3rd row.

3   11/0 Delicas with one 15/0 slipped on Row 2 and then on every row, (alternating 3 gold and 3 black).

4   11/0 Delica's with 15/0's slipped on. Work Rows 1 and 2 plain, ***Row 3** slip on one, **Row 4** slip on 2, **Row 5** slip on 1, **Rows 6 and 7**, plain*.
Repeat pattern from * to *. Use a tight tension.

1 (above) & 2 (below) shown at 200%

DIAG 1

1ST ROW: Diag 1 - Start with a ladder stitch base of four beads.

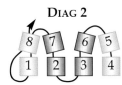

DIAG 2

2ND ROW: Diag 2 - Coming out of the top of end bead 4 (*you may need to turn your ladder*), add two beads and go into bead 3. Come out of bead 2, add two beads and go into bead 1. To position yourself for the next row, go into bead 8. Your thread will be on the outside of bead 1.

DIAG 3

3RD ROW: Diag 3 - As for row 2, add beads in pairs and position yourself for the next row.

DIAG 4

TO END: Diag 4 - Continue working in this manner for desired length and close up the end of the bracelet by ladder stitching the last row together.

Weave and tie off the thread ends into the work, hiding the knots.

VARIATIONS - SLIDING ON AN ACCENT BEAD OR TWO

This will distort the edges of the beading a little, particularly when decreasing, as you will need a much tighter tension to close the beading up. See enlarged pictures of designs 3 and 4 below.

DIAG5

DIAG 6

Herringbone

BY MARY MOTT

MATERIALS USED
3mm Cubes
Nymo D Thread
John James 10 Short Blunt
Beading Needle
Ring & Toggle Clasp

Instructions are on page 22.

STEP 1: Make a ladder of 6 cubes. *DIAG 1 page 23.*

STEP 2: Work Herringbone Stitch to desired length. *DIAG 2 & 3 page 23* and ladder stitch the last row together. *Diag 4.*

STEP 3: Taper the ends of the bracelet. *The easiest way to do this is using Brick Stitch. See Diagram 5 below.*

STEP 4: Thread up three beads on toggle end and one bead on ring end *(DIAG 6 below)* and attach clasps.

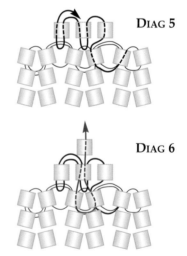

DIAG 5

DIAG 6

Herringbone Bracelet

BY JILL OXTON

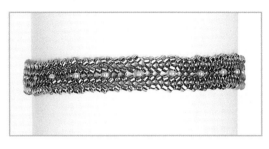

MATERIALS USED

		QTY
★	11/0 Delica DBR31 Gold	290
■	11/0 Delica DBR507 Purple	286
◎	15/0 Mill Hill 40123 Cream	19

Gold Nymo D Thread

John James 10 Short Blunt Beading Needle

Ring & Toggle & findings

Diagrams and instructions are on page 22.

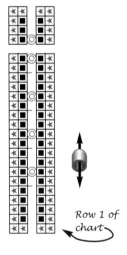

Row 1 of chart

CHART MARKINGS

Ignore blank areas on chart, this is to make space for slip on beads.

The symbol indicates the row that you slip on the bead.

The small red line on the chart indicates the position the slipped on bead will sit.

The top end of the chart shows how to end after the last slip-on bead.

Row 1: Make a ladder of 4 DBR31 beads. *DIAG 1 page 23.*

Pick up two DBR's at a time.

Rows 2 to 6: Work 1 gold 1 Purple; 1 purple 1 gold. *DIAG 2 page 23.*

Row 7: Work 1 gold 1 purple; *slip on 15/0;* 1 purple 1 gold. *See Diagram 5 on page 23.*

Row 8 to 10: Work 1 gold 1 purple; 1 purple 1 gold.

Row 11: Work 1 gold 1 purple; *slip on 15/0;* 1 purple 1 gold.

Repeat Rows 8 to 11 until 3 rows shorter than desired length.

To end: Repeat Row 8 twice.

Repeat Row 1, once.

Weave in thread end and attach findings.

Herringbone Spiral

BY MARY MOTT

MATERIALS USED

4 grams 11/0 DBR611 Dark Plum
4 grams 11/0 Seed Bead
Wine Nymo D Thread
John James 10 Short Blunt
Beading Needle
Ring & Toggle Clasp

Additional instructions are on page 22.

STEP 1: *DIAGRAM 1* - Make a two drop ladder DBR's *(6 pairs, 12 beads)* and join ladder to make a cylinder.

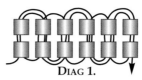

DIAG 1.

NOTE THAT OUR DIAGRAMS ARE FLAT, BUT THIS STITCH IS WORKED IN THE ROUND.

STEP 2: *DIAGRAM 2* - With the needle pointing up from the last pair, pick up 1 x DBR and 1 x seed bead. *Go down into the next bead to the left and then up from the following bead to the left. Pick up 1 x DBR and 1 x seed bead*, repeat once more from * to * going down into the next bead and up out the the following bead **and** the first bead of this row.

DIAG 2

DIAG 2A

Diagram 2A gives you an idea of what it looks like in the round at Step 2.

STEP 3: *DIAGRAM 3* - Pick up 1 x DBR and 1 x seed bead. Go down through the next left (which is a seed bead) and up through 2 DBR's. Repeat to end of round.

DIAG 3:

STEP 4: *DIAGRAM 4* - Pick up 1 x DBR and 1 x seed bead. Go down through the next left (which is a seed bead) and up through 3 DBR's. Repeat to end of round.

DIAG 4:

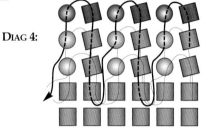

STEP 5: Repeat Step 4 to desired length, finishing with two rounds of DBR's.

Attach clasps using a new length of thread.

Start and Finish off Threads

Weave in thread ends, by weaving up the column of beads, knotting between beads and pulling the knot inside a bead to hide it.

Needle Weaving

BY DI NOYCE

MATERIALS

Base Cords - we used 4 strands of Sanshi Silk Thread No. 43 *(a similar thickness to No.12 Pearl Cotton)* or use 8 strands of Nymo D.

Nymo D Thread to match.

Assortment of beads, seed and bugle beads in different sizes colours and shapes.

John James No. 10 Short Blunt Beading Needle.

Ring & Toggle Clasp

METHOD

1 Cut four cords double the length required, **plus** 25cms (10").

2 Pass the cords through the loop of one of the findings (Diagram 1).

3 Keeping the two bundles of four cords separate, knot the ends of each group of four threads together, to make it easier to keep the cords even.

4 Thread the needle with Nymo D in a colour to compliment the base cords and the bead colours.

5   Lay the thread alongside one of the bundles of four cords. Starting next to the loop of the finding, make several tight *figure eight* weaves around and through the two bundles of cords to anchor the thread. (Diagrams 2a to 2e).

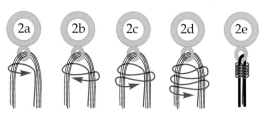

6   Work *figure eight* weaves and start adding beads, using the smaller beads first and gradually building up to the larger beads and bugles. *Diagram 3.*

The beads will slide to the back and the sides to cover the base cords.

Add one bead every two or three *figure eight* weaves.

7   Every six beads or so, loop the thread around one of the base bundles and pass needle through the loop to anchor everything in place. *Diagram 4.*

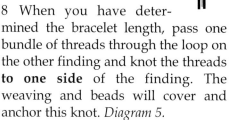

8   When you have determined the bracelet length, pass one bundle of threads through the loop on the other finding and knot the threads **to one side** of the finding. The weaving and beads will cover and anchor this knot. *Diagram 5.*

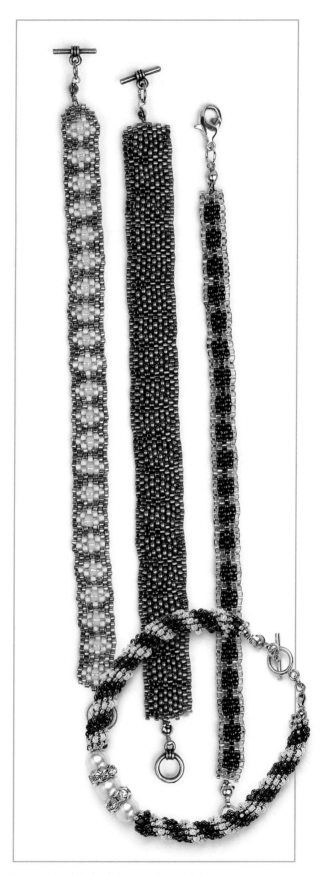

Peyote Stitch

Peyote Stitch is one of the most common off loom stitches with the beads lying off centre to each other.

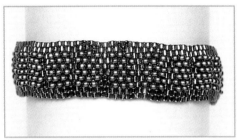

Even Count

Odd Count

Odd Count

Spiral

PEYOTE STITCH
EVEN COUNT - FLAT
(This is not symmetrical)

START: Cut thread as long as you can manage it and tie a waste bead onto the end, leaving a tail of about 15cm (6"). *The waste bead is not part of the beading and will be removed later.*

STEP 1: String up an even number of beads. *This will be rows 1 and 2*

STEP 2: To start row 3, pick up a bead and pass the needle through the second bead from the end. Bead 9 on our diagram.

STEP 3: Pick up the next bead, miss one bead on the previous row and take your needle through bead 7. Continue in this manner to the end of the row.

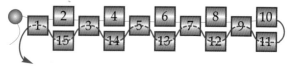

STEP 4: Work back in the opposite direction, missing one bead and going into the next.

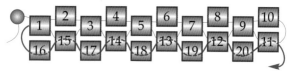

COUNTING THE ROWS

Rows in peyote stitch are counted diagonally. Following a chart can be confusing, therefore we have *"easy to read"* charts for our projects.

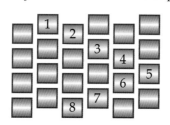

PEYOTE STITCH
ODD COUNT - FLAT - *Symmetrical*

START: Cut thread as long as you can manage it and tie a waste bead onto the end, leaving a tail of about 15cm (6"). *The waste bead is not part of the beading and will be removed later.*

STEP 1: String up an odd number of beads.

Note that these strung up beads will be rows 1 and 2

STEP 2: To turn for row 3, pick up a bead and pass the needle through the second bead from the end. Bead 4 on our diagram.

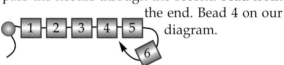

STEP 3: Pick up the next bead, miss one bead on the previous row and take your needle through bead 2. Continue in this manner to the end of the row.

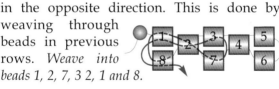

STEP 4: To turn you will need to get your thread into the correction position to work back in the opposite direction. This is done by weaving through beads in previous rows. *Weave into beads 1, 2, 7, 3 2, 1 and 8.*

Then work back, missing one bead and going into the next and continue in this manner.

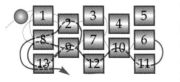

The next and subsequent left side turns will be easier as you only have to weave through beads 8, 9, 2, 8 & 13. *As my tension was a little tighter on the weave side, I now make a small weave on the other side to compensate.*

HELPFUL HINTS ON PEYOTE STITCH

Nymo D thread wears more and in fact broke using peyote stitch. I now use *"smoke" 4lb Fireline,* a fishing line available from Woolworths that is easy to handle and knot but stronger than Nymo D.

You will find it much easier to work peyote stitch, if you first work a practice strip about 17cm to 18cm wide using size 11/0 beads. You can then use this as a base to work any peyote designs that are not as wide as your practice strip. This will also give you a firmer tension at the start.

With this method you do not thread up the first two rows of beads at the same time, but work the first and second row separately.

As you are working on one row, you may find that you are unable to add the last bead on the first row. I skip this bead and work down the next row **adding it and the bead beside** it when I get to that end again *using Brick Stitch,* I then weave around to position myself for the following row.

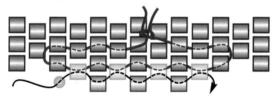

1   Thread up the first row of the design onto the edge of the *peyote strip (blue beads on our diagram)* using a thread a different colour to that you will be using for the design.

Tie the ends into a knot on top of the beading to secure. This will be cut off later.

2   Cut working thread and tie a stopper bead 15cm (6") from the end. Thread through first bead of first row and work the second row.

3   Work the third row and then the remainder of the design.

3   Remove the beading from the *peyote strip* by cutting the coloured thread and separating the two pieces.

4   Remove stopper bead and weave in thread end.

ODD COUNT PEYOTE TENSION

When working odd count Peyote, my tension was tighter on the edge of the peyote, where I did all the weaving to get the needle into the correction position to exit the bead.

To achieve a more even tension, I am now making a weave on the other edge (even though technically speaking, it is not required).

Pink Diamond

BY JILL OXTON

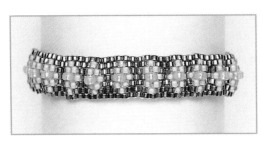

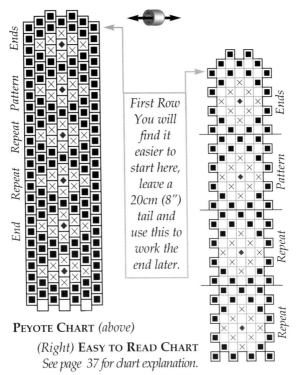

First Row You will find it easier to start here, leave a 20cm (8″) tail and use this to work the end later.

PEYOTE CHART *(above)*

(Right) **EASY TO READ CHART**
See page 37 for chart explanation.

REQUIREMENTS FOR A **16** CM LENGTH   QTY

■	11/0 DBR 507 *Metallic Blend**
✕	11/0 MG 7032 *Pink**
◆	8/0 Mill Hill 18819 *Pink*

Ring & Toggle
2 x Cover tips
2 x 3mm Jump rings

The Pink Diamond Bracelet was worked using odd count Peyote with Nymo D thread and a John James #10 Short Blunt Beading Needle.

For a **16cm** (6¹⁄₂″) length we worked 22 pattern repeats and painted the back of the pink diamond areas with nail polish to keep them raised.

*MG = Maria George Pty Ltd; DBR = Miyuki Delica

Even Count Peyote

BY JILL OXTON

The Even Count Bracelet was worked in peyote stitch using 11/0 Czech beads, 11/0 Delica's, Gold Nymo D thread and a John James 10 Short Blunt Beading Needle.

Because we used two different types of beads, the seed beads being slightly larger than the Delica's, the areas worked with the seed beads stood proud.

To encourage this, when the bracelet was completed we painted the back of the seed bead sections with several coats of clear nail varnish.

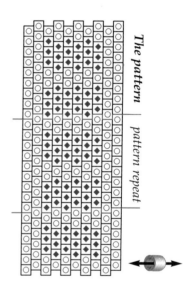

The pattern

pattern repeat

REQUIREMENTS FOR
16 CM LENGTH

◯	600 x 11/0 Delica's
◆	360 x 11/0 Czech

Nymo D thread
Ring & Toggle
2 x Cover tips
2 x 3mm Jump rings

Easy to Read Chart

The hardest thing about working Peyote Stitch is following the chart.

For those of you that also find this difficult, I have recharted the graph, so you can easily read the chart row by row.

The Easy to Read Chart shows the actual horizontal position of the beads, but does not show the correct vertical position.

The red lines on the chart indicate the pattern repeats.

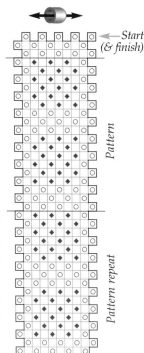

Start (& finish)

Pattern

Pattern repeat

THE PATTERN

Cut thread as long as you can manage it (about 2 metres (80")). Pull thread very firmly.

Rows 1 & 2: Start by threading up 10 x 11/0 DBR's *(or use waste strip method on page 34).*

Row 3: 5 x DBR.

Row 4: 1 x DBR, 3 x Czech, 1 x DBR.

Row 5: 1 x DBR, 3 x Czech, 1 x DBR.

Row 6: 1 x DBR, 3 x Czech, 1 x DBR.

Row 7: 1 x DBR, 3 x Czech, 1 x DBR.

Row 8: 1 x DBR, 3 x Czech, 1 x DBR.

Row 9: 1 x DBR, 3 x Czech, 1 x DBR.

Row 10: 5 x DBR.

Row 11: 5 x DBR.

Row 12: 5 x DBR.

Repeat Rows 4 to 12 until bracelet is the desired length.

THE CHART

The pattern repeats itself on the bracelet every two rectangles (red sections) on the chart. We worked 19 rectangles and finished with three rows of peyote in the same colour as the edge.

Odd Count
Peyote
BY JILL OXTON

The Odd Count Bracelet was worked in peyote stitch using 10/0 Czech beads, 11/0 Delica's, Wine Nymo D thread and a John James 10 Short Blunt Beading Needle.

Because we used two different types of beads, the seed beads being slightly larger than the Delica's, the areas worked with the seed beads stood proud.

To encourage this, we worked with a very tight tension

REQUIREMENTS FOR
16 CM LENGTH

○ 400 x 11/0 Delica's

◆ 168 x 10/0 Czech

Nymo D thread
Ring & Toggle
2 x Cover tips
2 x 3mm Jump rings

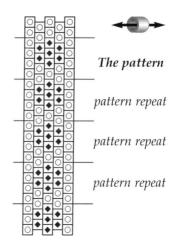

The pattern

pattern repeat

pattern repeat

pattern repeat

EASY TO READ CHART

I find the hardest thing about working Peyote Stitch is following the chart.

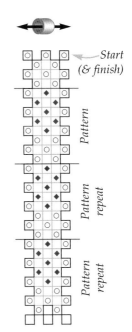

For those of you that also find this difficult, I have recharted the graph, so you can easily read the chart row by row.

The Easy to Read Chart shows the correct horizontal position of the beads, but not the correct vertical position.

The red lines on the chart indicate the pattern repeats.

THE PATTERN

Cut thread as long as you can manage it (about 2 metres (80")). Pull thread very firmly.

Rows 1 & 2: Start by threading up 5 x 11/0 DBR's *(or use waste strip method above)*.

Row 3:   3 x DBR.

Row 4:   2 x DBR.

Row 5:   1 x DBR, 1 x Czech, 1 x DBR.

Row 6:   2 x Czech.

Row 7:   1 x DBR, 1 x Czech, 1 x DBR.

Row 8:   2 x Czech.

Row 9:   1 x DBR, 1 x Czech, 1 x DBR.

Row 10: 2 x DBR.

Row 11: 3 x DBR.

Repeat Rows 4 to 11 until bracelet is the desired length.

THE CHART

The pattern repeats itself on the bracelet every square (red section) on the chart. We worked 19 rectangles and finished with four rows of DBR.

PEYOTE SPIRAL
ODD COUNT TUBULAR PEYOTE

Using an odd number of beads makes tubular peyote spiral down the tube. Therefore there will not be a straight edge on the top or the bottom and the bead you are working will always be slightly lower than the others.

You will need a form to work around. Depending on how wide your tube is, you can use skewers, knitting needles and dowels. Sand any wooden objects well, so that the thread does not snag on them.

For our spiral bracelet we used a wooden satay stick about 15cm (6″) long, well sanded and painted with several coats of clear nail varnish.

While you are working the spiral, check that the thread does not wrap around the form.

Worked firmly and worked from left to right, or right to left.

STEP 1: Cut two metres of thread and leaving a 15cm (6″) tail, string up an **odd** number of beads to fit snugly in a circle around the form.

Pass the thread through all of these beads twice, exiting from the first bead strung *(at the tail)*.

Place circle of beads over form and pull thread taut.

STEP 2: String one bead and pass needle and thread through the third bead of the first round.

Continue adding one bead to every second bead all around and you find that you start to spiral.

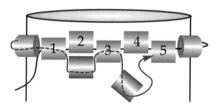

STEP 2: Continue in this manner for the desired length.

Peyote Spiral

BY JILL OXTON

The Peyote Spiral Bracelet was worked using odd count peyote stitch, with Green Nymo D thread and a John James 10 Short Blunt Beading Needle.

We used a well sanded wooden satay stick as our form.

REQUIREMENTS FOR **16** CM LENGTH	QTY
11/0 **Czech** *Purple/Green True Cut*	240
11/0 **Pearl** Seed Bead *Mill Hill 00123*	120
15/0 **Gold** Seed Bead *Mill Hill 40557*	240
2 x *8mm diameter* Gold & Diamontee Rondells	
3 x *7mm diameter* Round Pearl Beads	
2 x *3mm diameter* Round Gold Beads	
Ring & Toggle; 2 x Cover tips	
2 x 3mm Jump rings	

THE PATTERN

1   Thread up 9 x 15/0 Gold - see Step 1 on page 40.

2   Work the beads in the following order - Czech, ***Gold, Pearl, Gold, 2 x Czech,*** Gold, Pearl, Gold, 2 x Czech. Repeat from * to * for 6.5cm and end with 9 x Gold.

3   Work a second spiral the same.

ASSEMBLE THE BRACELET

4   Using four strands of Nymo D thread, run thread through cover tip, 15/0 Gold; 3mm Gold; Spiral Tube; Pearl; Rondell; Pearl; Rondell; Pearl; Spiral Tube; 3mm Gold; 15/0 Gold; covertip; 15/0 gold and back again.

Place another 15/0 on the thread, knot ends together tightly.

Paint knot with nail polish, close cover tips and attach ring and toggle (or clasp) to cover tip using jump rings.

We worked our Right Angle Weave (RAW) using 4mm squares, triangles and Japanese seed beads.

Right Angle Weave

Right Angle Weave is a useful stitch for constructing three dimensional items and for edgings, straps and bracelets. Different types and sizes of beads can completely change the look of a simple RAW chain.

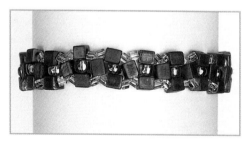

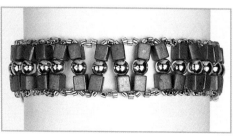

RIGHT ANGLE WEAVE (RAW)

Right Angle Weave is a very useful stitch for bracelets and straps for amulet bags worked one or two rows wide.

You will get a squarer shape using round seed beads rather than cylinder beads. RAW can also be worked using bugle beads.

Our diagrams show one bead per side, but you can use two or more beads per side.

Right angle weave or RAW, is worked clockwise and anti-clockwise. If your previous circle was worked clockwise then your next circle will be worked anti-clockwise and vice versa. Our instructions reflect the direction of our diagrams.

FIRST ROW/ MAKING A CHAIN

1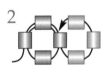

1 Leaving a tail of 15cm (6″) for weaving in later, string up four beads. Run the thread through the first three beads again to form a circle. Pull the thread taut so the beads are touching.

2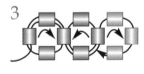

2 Pick up three beads on your needle and working anti-clockwise, bring the needle and thread back though the last vertical bead *(called **the connecting bead**)* and the first two beads just added. You should now have two squares.

3

3 Add three more beads. Working clockwise, take the needle and thread through the connecting bead in the previous square *(the last bead you came through in the previous square)* and the first two beads just added. You should now have three squares.

4 Alternate steps 2 and 3 until your chain is the desired length.

Second & subsequent rows

5 Add three beads. Working anticlockwise, pass the needle through the last horizontal bead of the previous row.

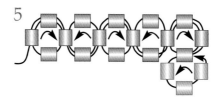

6 Add two beads. Working clockwise, pass the needle through the horizontal bead of the previous row and the last vertical bead of the previous square. Continue working in this manner to the end of the row.

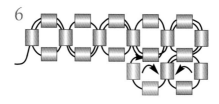

Joining two pieces together

The green beads indicate beads that need to be added when joining two pieces.

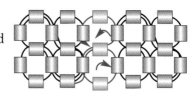

Filling in or embellishing RAW

When all RAW is complete, it can be filled in or embellished using the same or a contrasting bead *(the green bead in our diagram)*. Use one strand of Nymo D when working the RAW and filling in, as this extra step can cause thread build up.

Work from left to right, or right to left.

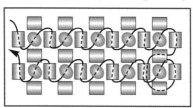

RAW Daisy Bracelet

BY JILL OXTON

This is the first row of RAW worked using two beads per side and embellished in every alternate square with a larger seed bead.

MATERIALS WE USED

11/0 Japanese Seed Beads in gold and silver
8/0 Seed Bead Mill Hill 18221
Nymo D Thread
John James 10 Tapestry Pointed Short Beading Needle

STEP 1: Leaving a 6″ tail of thread, pick up 8 x 11/0 gold beads and run thread through the first six beads again to form a circle.

STEP 2: Pick up 6 x 11/0 silver beads and working anti-clockwise, bring needle and thread back through two vertical beads on the side and the first four beads just added. You should now have two squares.

REPEAT STEP 2, in 11/0 gold beads, then alternate 11/0 silver and gold.

STEP 3: Embellish every second square using 8/0 seed beads.

Finish off thread ends by weaving them into the RAW making several slip knots along the way to secure the thread.
Use a new piece of thread to attach findings (see pages 11 & 104).

RAW Pearl Bracelet

BY JILL OXTON

This is the first row of RAW worked using three beads per side and embellished in every square with a pearl.

MATERIALS WE USED
11/0 Japanese Seed Beads in gold, silver, black and bronze.
25 x 3mm diameter Pearl beads.
1 x 6mm diameter Pearl for clasp.
Nymo D Thread.
John James 10 Tapestry Pointed Short Beading Needle.

Step 1: Leaving a 6″ tail of thread, pick up *1 silver, 1 gold, 1 black* repeat from * to * 3 times and run thread through the first eight beads again to form a circle.

Step 2: Pick up *1 bronze, 1 silver, 1 gold* repeat from * to * twice, then pick up one bronze and working anti-clockwise, bring needle and thread back through two vertical beads on the side and the first six beads just added. You should now have two squares.

Step 3: Repeat Step 2 using black beads instead of bronze beads and alternate Steps 2 and 3 until desired length. Embellish with pearl beads.

Finish off thread ends by weaving them into the RAW making several slip knots along the way to secure the thread, then using a new piece of thread, attach the 6mm pearl bead on one end and a beaded loop on the other.

RAW Square Bracelet

BY JILL OXTON

This is the first row of RAW worked using two beads per side and embellished in every square with a larger seed bead.

MATERIALS WE USED

Miyuki 4mm Squares - 134FR
11/0 Triangles - 11
8/0 Seed Bead Mill Hill - 16024
Nymo D Thread - Champagne
John James 10 Tapestry Pointed
Short Beading Needle

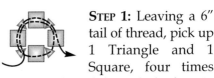

STEP 1: Leaving a 6" tail of thread, pick up 1 Triangle and 1 Square, four times and run thread through the first six beads again to form a circle.

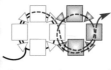

STEP 2: Pick up 1 Triangle, then 1 square and one triangle three times. Working anti-clockwise, bring needle and thread back through one square bead (on the side) and the first four beads just added. You should now have two squares.

STEP 3: Repeat Step 2, clockwise and then Steps 2 and 3 until the bracelet is the desired length (about 16cm).

STEP 4: Embellish every square using 8/0 seed beads.

The coloured beads on the diagram indicate the beads the thread weaves through.

Finish off thread ends by weaving them into the RAW making several slip knots along the way to secure the thread. Use a new piece of thread to attach findings *(see pages 11 & 104).*

Slinky RAW Bracelet

BY ERIKA BARNA

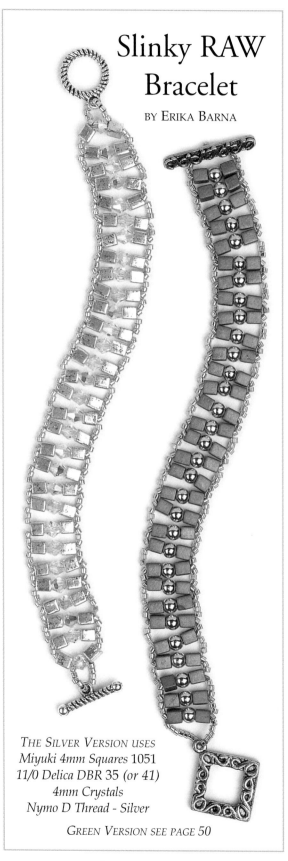

THE SILVER VERSION USES
Miyuki 4mm Squares 1051
11/0 Delica DBR 35 (or 41)
4mm Crystals
Nymo D Thread - Silver

GREEN VERSION SEE PAGE 50

Slinky RAW Bracelet

by Erika Barna

MATERIALS - GREEN VERSION

62 x 4mm Miyuki Squares 2035
206 x 11/0 Miyuki Delica DBR 34 *(or 42)*
31 x 4mm Accent Bead or Crystal
Ring & Toggle Bracelet Clasp
Nymo D Thread - Gold
John James 10 Tapestry Pointed Short Beading
Needle

The bracelet is worked in Right Angle Weave using three different sized beads. The ring and toggle clasps are attached to the ends of the bracelet with a loop of 11/0 cylinder beads. For more strength use two strands of Nymo D.

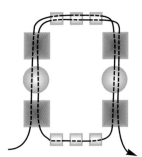

1 Leaving a tail of 15cm (8") for weaving in later, string up 1 x Square, 1 x Accent, 1 x Square, 3 x DBR, 1 x Square, 1 x Accent, 1 x Square, 3 x DBR. Run the thread through the first nine beads again to form a circle. Pull the thread taut so the beads are touching.

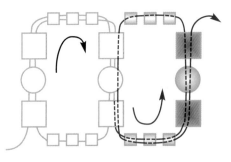

2 Pick up 3 x DBR, 1 x Square, 1 x Accent, 1 x Square, 3 x DBR and bring the needle and thread back though the last vertical Square, Accent, Square *(called the connecting beads)* and the first six beads just added. You should now have two squares.

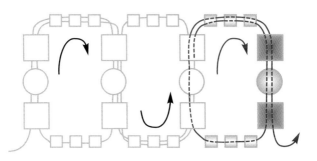

3 Add 3 x DBR, 1 x Square, 1 x Accent, 1 x Square, 3 x DBR. Working clockwise, take the needle and thread through the three connecting beads in the previous square (*the last three beads you came through in the previous square*) and the first six beads just added. You should now have three squares.

Alternate steps 2 and 3 until your chain is the desired length. Weave thread ends into the bracelet, making several slip knots along the way.

Using a new double strand of thread and coming out of the end of the bracelet, add 5 DBR's, go through ring of clasp, add 5 DBR's. *Check you can close the bracelet* and then run thread through all clasp beads again for strength and finish off thread ends.

Helpful Hint

The 11/0 Delica's tend to slip inside some of the 4mm squares. This gives a V type pattern to the rungs. For a straighter rung, use 11/0 seed beads, which are slightly larger than Delica's and will not slip through the hole in the squares. Alternately, you could use 1 x 11/0, 1 x 8/0, 1 x 11/0 seed beads in matching colours instead of the 11/0 Delica's.

Spiral Rope

This simple yet decorative stitch has many uses. Quickly worked up, it can be used for bracelets, straps, belts, earrings and necklaces.

Use any combination of beads and bead sizes or add an accent bead and/or spacer between the sections

The focal point of Autumn Spiral is a large gemstone used as the toggle.

SPIRAL ROPE

STEP 1: Pick up four core beads and three main colour (outside) beads. Draw them down to the end of your thread, leaving a tail of about 10cm (4") to be woven in later.

The thread tail is now the bottom of the chain and the working end is the top.

STEP 2: Pass your needle back through the four core beads, from the bottom to the top and pull the thread to form an irregular loop.

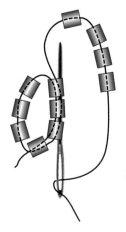

STEP 3: Pick up one core bead and three outside beads. Pass your needle through the last three core beads added in Step 1.

STEP 4: Pass your needle through the single core bead added in Step 3 and pull thread firmly. *The core bead should now be sitting on top of the other core beads.*

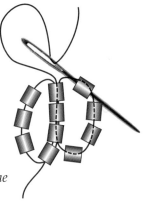

STEP 5: Adjust the outside beads just added so they are sitting snugly next to the previous outside row.

STEP 6: Repeat Steps 3, 4 & 5 until your chain is the desired length.

It will take a few repetitions before spiral rope stitch becomes evident, but each new row of outside (blue) beads should be one bead higher than the previous row.

Start and finish off thread by weaving into the spirals and core, making several knots along the way.

ADDING EMBELLISHMENT BEADS

To add embellishment bead(s) to the spiral rope as we did for the Rose Amulet pictured left and the green bracelet on page 58, work spiral rope for the desired length then add the embellishment bead(s) and/or spacers, pushing them snug to the spiral rope.

Pick up four core beads and three spiral beads and push them up tightly against the embellishment bead(s) then pass the needle back up through the four core beads to make the first spiral of this section.

Now reinforce the stitching by passing the needle back down the new spiral, the embellishment bead(s) and the last spiral of the previous section, then weave back up through the core beads, the large bead and the new core beads, to be in position to continue working the next spiral rope section.

Gunmetal Blue

BY JILL OXTON

Gunmetal Blue Earrings

MATERIALS WE USED

48 x Core Beads DBR35

38 x Outside Beads* - 6mm Bugle Bead

Blue Nymo D Thread

John James 10 Short Blunt Beading Needle

2 x Silver Shepherds Hooks

2 x Silver Cover tips

2 x 3mm Jump Rings

STEP 1: Pick up 4 x DBR6 for core and 1 bugle for outside row

STEP 2: Same as instructions on page 54.

STEP 3: Pick up 1 x DBR6 (core bead) and 1 x bugle and then pass your needle through the last FOUR core beads added in Step 1.

STEP 4, 5 & 6: Same as instructions on page 54.

NOTE: The Bugle beads used were approximately 1/4" in length (the length of 4 Delica's and about the same diameter).

SPIRAL ROPE CHAIN is a very quick and pretty stitch to use for necklaces, earrings, bracelets and chains for bags.

We worked the Gunmetal bracelet using 11/0 Delica cylinder beads in two colours.

You will use three times as many beads for the outside colour as you use for the core. We used about 60 Delica's in the outside colour and 20 Delica's in the core colour per 2.5 cm (1").

Use a John James #10 Short Blunt Beading Needle with Nymo D thread and cut your thread as long as you can manage it.

START AND END THREADS by weaving them back down through the spiral as far as you can, through the core and outside beads. Knot your thread at least once around the core beads and then pass it through at least five more beads before cutting the thread.

It is very easy to embellish this stitch using different sized and irregular shaped beads in any colour scheme you desire.

BUGLE BEADS were used for the earrings and look very effective as a drop, but a bracelet made in spiral rope using bugles would not bend nicely.

Gunmetal Blue Bracelet

MATERIALS WE USED
Miyuki Delica 11/0 Cylinder Beads (DBR)
     128 x Core Beads DBR35 Silver
     384 x Outside Beads DBR6 Gunmetal
Blue Nymo D Thread
John James 10 Short Blunt Beading Needle
1 x Silver Bracelet Clasp
2 x Silver Cover tips
2 x 3mm Jump Rings
Bead quantities above are for a 16cm length.

Green Spiral

The green spiral bracelet was worked in spiral rope following the instructions on page 54.

The core bead was DBR604.

The outside beads were a bead soup mixture *by Jenny Knight* of green beads, made up of chips, drops and assorted sizes of round and seed beads, picked up at random.

6mm diameter Silver Spacers and 6mm diameter round beads were also strung onto the bracelet between segments of spiral rope.

We worked *five spirals and then added a silver spacer, 6mm bead, silver spacer*. Repeat for the desired length of the bracelet, ending with five spiral rope stitches.

See page 55 for "Adding Embellishment Beads to Spiral Rope".

BEAD MIX BY JENNY KNIGHT

Blue Spiral

The blue spiral bracelet was worked in spiral rope following the instructions on page 54.

The core bead was an 11/0 Delica DBR512 - Silver.

The outside beads were:

11/0 Delica DBR325 - Blue

3.4 mm Miyuki Drop 401F

Mill Hill 8/0 Seed Bead No. 18027 Caspian Blue.

Method

Spiral 1: 3 x DBR.

Spiral 2: 1 x DBR, 1 x Drop, 1 x DBR.

Spiral 3: 3 x DBR

Spiral 4: 1 x DBR, 1 x 8/0, 1 x DBR

Repeat Spirals 1 to 4 until bracelet is the desired length.

Autumn Spiral

The autumn spiral bracelet was worked in spiral rope following the instructions on page 54.

The core beads were 11/0 DBR's. **The outside beads** were a mixture of autumn shaded beads *by Jenny Knight,* made up of chips, drops and assorted small round and seed beads.

The outside beads were picked up at random when working the spiral.

The bracelet closure was a toggle shaped gemstone chip on one end and a beaded loop on the other end.

BEAD MIX BY JENNY KNIGHT

Gallery

WIRE BRACELETS BY **JO GARDNER**

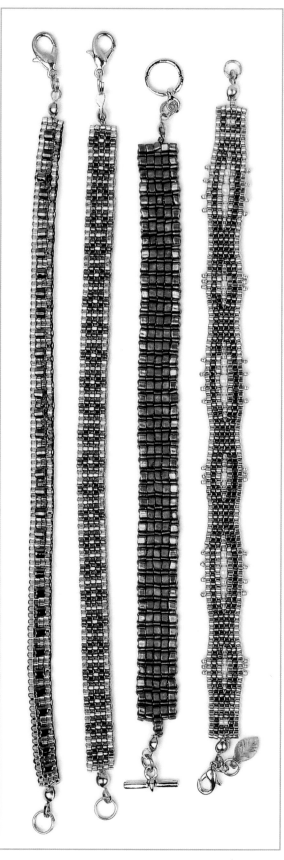

Page 62 - Jill Oxton's Beautiful Bracelets

Square Stitch

Square Stitch is a very strong stitch that is ideal for use with charted designs and works particularly well with Japanese cylinder beads

It can be used for bracelets, belts, barrettes, spectacle chains, purses, bags, boxes, pots and picture beading.

The method we have given in this book is ideal for bracelets, but for items wider than 2.5cm (1") we would not recommend running the thread back through the beading after each row as it can distort and buckle the beading.

11/0 Triangles

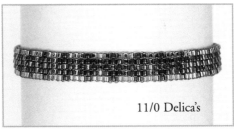

11/0 Delica's

4mm Squares

SQUARE STITCH

(RIGID METHOD SUITABLE FOR BRACELETS)

BLUE DIAGRAMS ARE RIGHT HANDED.

GREEN DIAGRAMS ARE LEFT HANDED

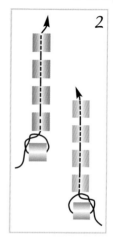

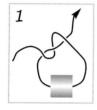

To Start: Cut your thread about 2 metres (80") long and thread needle.

Diagram 1: Tie a stopper bead onto the tail end of the thread. Don't knot, as this bead will be removed later. It's purpose is to stop your beads falling off the thread. Leave a tail of at least 10cm (4"), this will be woven into the beading later.

The First Row *Diagram 2:* Following the pattern, string up the first row of beads from the bottom to the top.

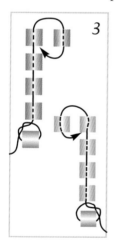

The Second Row *Diagram 3:* (*Right handers work clockwise, left handers work anti-clockwise*).

The second row will be your hardest row as you are attaching beads to beads that can slide about. Use your stopper bead to adjust the tension when working this row.

continued on page 65

The Second Row *continued*

Following the colours in the pattern, pick up one bead. Leave it on your needle and pass the needle from the bottom to the top of the last bead and then back down from the top to the bottom of the new bead *Diagram 4.*

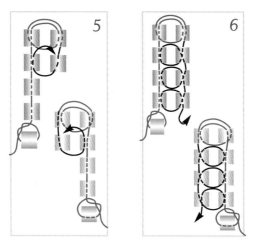

Diagram 5: *Pick up a bead and attach it to the adjacent bead in the previous column by passing the needle from the bottom to top through the bead and then top to bottom through the new bead*.

Repeat this step to the end of the row.

Diagram 6: This shows the second row finished.

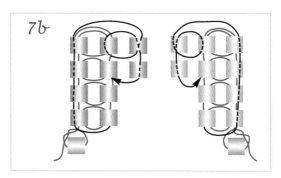

The Third Row *Diagram 7B*: Run the thread back up through the previous row *(the row before the row just worked)* and then work from the top down on the next row.

Your thread will lie on top of the bead of the row just completed. Although a little less perfect than method 7C on page 66, this is the safest method for beginners to use until you can judge by feel how many thread passes a bead will take.

SQUARE STITCH
(RIGID METHOD SUITABLE FOR BRACELETS)

continued from page 65

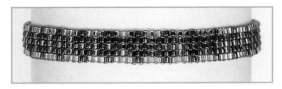

The worst thing you can do when beading is to pack your beads with so much thread that you cannot make any more passes to finish and start threads and attach findings or other embellishments. You will learn in time to judge by feel whether the bead is getting too packed with thread, but it does take a little practice and you will break a few beads before you can safely judge this.

When my needle gets stuck in the beading I will use a pair of pliers to help me pull it through. Occasionally I break a bead, but I have learned to judge whether the bead will take the extra pressure or not.

One of the things to watch is that Black Nymo D is thicker for instance than Silver Nymo D and some other colours, so I would be able to make more thread passes with silver Nymo D than Black.

Diagram 7C below shows a tidier method for working a bracelet in square stitch, but it does involve more thread passes.

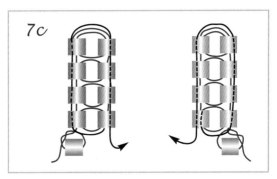

Diagram 7C: Run the thread back up through the previous row (*the row before the row just worked*) and then the row just worked. Turn your beading and work the next row.

I would not use method 7C when using 15/0 seed beads and other beads with smaller holes than 11/0 Delica's.

STARTING & FINISHING OFF THREADS IN SQUARE STITCH

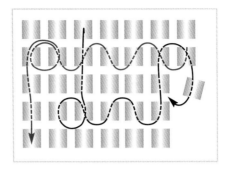

The red lines show finishing off the thread and the black lines show starting a new thread. You will need to weave in and out of at least five beads to secure the thread.

I never finish a thread on the end of a row, unless it is the end of the piece. I find that working two or three beads of the next row before finishing off the thread will ensure that I come out of the correct bead and am in the correct position to continue beading.

If you finish on the end of a row you may turn your work and inadvertently start on the wrong end which may give you a reflection line on your beading, as the beads stitched with the new thread will be sitting at a slightly different angle.

Start and finish off your threads at least one bead in from the edge. This will ensure that you do not cut any threads that are along the outside edge of the beading, and when you do cut the thread, you will not have a little whisker/end of the thread sticking out of from the edge of the bracelet. *This can be very annoying and is nearly impossible to trim.*

Trim your thread ends after the new thread has been added so you can pull the thread taut and tighten it up if it has been loosened a little when adding your new thread.

You can also leave a tail on your new thread to stop it slipping through the beads while you are weaving it into position.

When trimming your thread ends, pull the thread taut and then trim it. Any ends will slip inside the beads and/or will not be noticeable, **unless** they are on the outside edge.

Square Stitch Bracelet No. 1

by Di Noyce

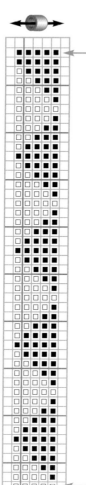

Thread up the first row of beads in the same direction as the arrow.

This bracelet was worked in square stitch and when each row was worked, running the thread back through the previous row and then the row that was just worked (method 7c) to make the beading firmer.

We used 11/0 Delica beads, Black Nymo D thread and a John James 10 Tapestry Pointed Short Beading Needle.

See page 64 for square stitch instructions.

Centre point for a 16cm length.

Miyuki Delica 11/0 Key

				Qty
■	DBR 10	■	Black	240
□	DBR 114	▨	Silver	230

Other Materials:
Nymo D - Black
2 x Silver Cover tips
1 x Silver Bracelet Clasp
2 x 3mm Jump Rings
Clear Nail Polish

Square Stitch Bracelet No 2

by Di Noyce

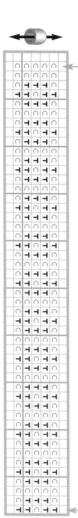

Thread up the first row of beads in the same direction as the arrow.

This bracelet was worked in square stitch and when each row was worked, running the thread back through the previous row and then the row that was just worked (method 7c) to make the beading firmer.

We used 11/0 Delica beads, Gold Nymo D thread and a John James 10 Tapestry Pointed Short Beading Needle.

See page 64 for square stitch instructions.

Centre point for a 16cm length.

Miyuki Delica 11/0 Key		Qty
■ DBR 135	Purple	234
C DBR 42	Gold	246

Other Materials:
Nymo D - Gold
2 x Gold Cover tips
1 x Gold Bracelet Clasp
2 x 3mm Gold Jump Rings
Clear Nail Polish

Embellished Bracelet

BY DI NOYCE

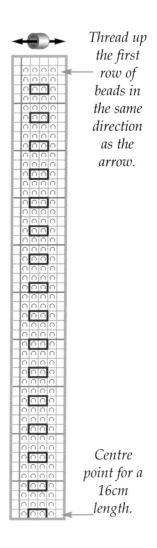

Thread up the first row of beads in the same direction as the arrow.

Centre point for a 16cm length.

We used 11/0 Delica beads, Nymo D thread and a John James 10 Tapestry Pointed Short Beading Needle.

See page 64 for square stitch instructions.

THE SILVER VERSION *used*

380 x 11/0 DBR 41 Silver

31 x 8/0 DBL 42 Gold

Embellished Ring

BY DI NOYCE

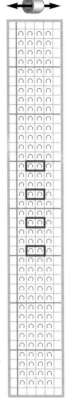

THE BRACELET was worked in square stitch using 11/0 Delica's. When each row was worked, the thread was run back through the previous row and then the row just worked.

On every third row the thread was run back through the previous row and then the row just worked, coming out one bead before the edge.

The 8/0 Delica was square stitched over the centre two beads and the thread was then run back through to the end of the row.

Square stitch three more rows in 11/0's and repeat until bracelet is the desired length, ending with two plain rows.

THE RING was worked in the same manner, but only four 8/0 Delica's were centred on the band.

Adjust the size to fit wearer by adding or subtracting rows.

MIYUKI DELICA 11/0		QTYB	QTYR
C DBR 42	Gold	380	152
MIYUKI DELICA 8/0			
DBL 5	Blue Iris	31	4

OTHER MATERIALS:
Nymo D - Gold
2 x Gold Cover tips
1 x Gold Bracelet Clasp
2 x 3mm Gold Jump Rings
Clear Nail Polish

Triangle Beads

Triangle beads act differently in square stitch. They do involve a little more work than the regular shaped beads as they turn and fit into each other and take up less space, but they do have some interesting effects.

The photo (right) shows the back and front of the Triangle Bracelet worked using three different shades of triangles. We used one colour for the border and worked in stripes using green and purple.

This gave us two different coloured bracelets in one, depending on which side you wear it.

Below is an example using triangle beads in two contrasting colours.

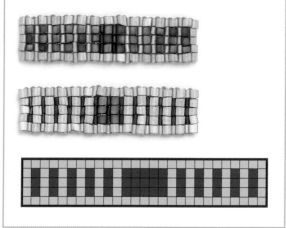

Triangle Bracelet

BY JILL OXTON

WORKED IN SQUARE STITCH.

Thread up the first row of beads in the same direction as the arrow.

This bracelet was worked in square stitch and when each row was worked, running the thread back through the previous row and then the row that was just worked (method 7c) to make the beading firmer.

We used 11/0 Triangles, Green Nymo D thread and a John James 10 Short Blunt Beading Needle.

See page 64 for square stitch instructions.

Centre point for a 16cm length.

11/0 TRIANGLES KEY		QTY
★	Bronze	198
☐	Matt Green Iris	144
•	Matt Pink Iris	138

OTHER MATERIALS:
Nymo D - Green
2 x Gold Cover tips
1 x Gold Bracelet Clasp
2 x 3mm Gold Jump Rings
Clear Nail Polish

Squares
in Square Stitch
BY JILL OXTON

These three bracelets were worked in square stitch using Miyuki 4mm Squares. Use two strands of Nymo D thread and a Short Blunt Beading Needle.

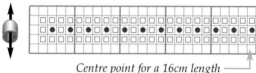

Centre point for a 16cm length ——

For the Bronze & Ruby Bracelet above we used:

☐ 118 x Miyuki 4mm Square #462 Bronze

● 23 x Miyuki 4mm Square#5 Ruby
   Wine Nymo D thread.

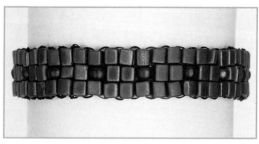

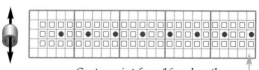

Centre point for a 16cm length ——

For the Blue Bracelet above we used:

☐ 126 x Miyuki 4mm Square #414FR Blue

● 15 x 6/0 Mill Hill Glass Seed Bead 16021
   Blue Nymo D thread.

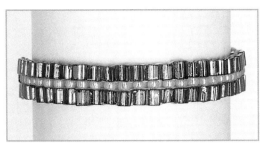

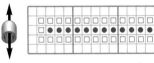

Centre point for a 16cm length ——————

For the Dusky Rose Bracelet above we used:

☐ 118 x Miyuki 4mm Square #12 Dusky Rose
● 15 x 8/0 Mill Hill 18819 Opal Blush
   Champagne Nymo D thread.

The Clasps *(also refer to pages 85 & 102).*

Above: The clasp was attached using a
cover tip and jump ring.

Above: The clasp was attached by slipping
a jump ring through the centre square.

Above: The clasp was attached by slipping
a jump ring through the centre square.

Confetti Bracelets

BY DI NOYCE

If you have unsorted 11/0 beads left over from previous projects you can put them to good use with these bracelets. Use a metallic colour for the outside edges and work the interior using beads picked up at random.

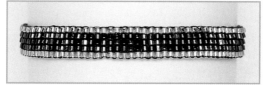

ABOVE THE BRACELETS ARE 5 BEADS HIGH AND USE AN 11/0 CYLINDER BEAD CONFETTI MIX AND DBR 42 SILVER LINED GOLD, FOR THE EDGES.

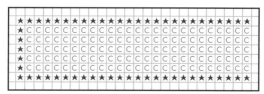

ABOVE THE BRACELET IS 7 BEADS HIGH AND USES A 11/0 CYLINDER BEAD CONFETTI MIX AND DBR 42 SILVER LINED GOLD, FOR THE EDGES.

Floating Beads

These use the same technique but have a different look, depending on the type, the size and the shape of the beads used.

The bottom two bracelets use a combination of square stitch and ladder stitch.

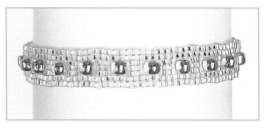

11/0 Delicas & 4mm Round Beads

11/0 Delicas & 4mm Squares

4mm Squares & 6mm Round Beads

8/0 Triangles & Crystal Buttons

Floating Beads

BY DI NOYCE

WORKED IN SQUARE STITCH.

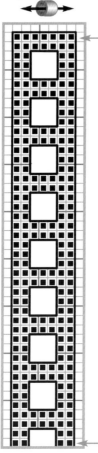

Thread up the first row of beads in the same direction as the arrow.

Similar in style to the Chunky Bracelet on page 82, this bracelet is worked solely in square stitch.

Square Stitch instructions are on page 64 and additional instructions for this method are on page 79.

Centre point for a 16cm length.

WE USED *(for a 16 cm length)*
460 x Miyuki 11/0 Delica's
17 x 4mm Round Beads
Nymo D
John James 10 Short Blunt Beading Needle

OTHER MATERIALS:
2 x Cover tips
1 Bracelet Clasp
2 Jump Rings
Clear Nail Polish

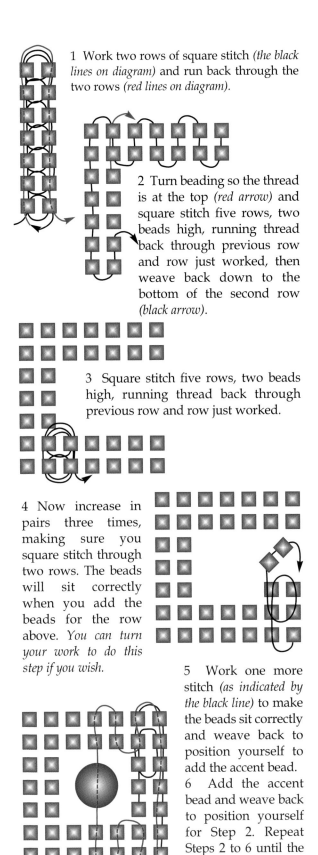

1 Work two rows of square stitch *(the black lines on diagram)* and run back through the two rows *(red lines on diagram)*.

2 Turn beading so the thread is at the top *(red arrow)* and square stitch five rows, two beads high, running thread back through previous row and row just worked, then weave back down to the bottom of the second row *(black arrow)*.

3 Square stitch five rows, two beads high, running thread back through previous row and row just worked.

4 Now increase in pairs three times, making sure you square stitch through two rows. The beads will sit correctly when you add the beads for the row above. *You can turn your work to do this step if you wish.*

5 Work one more stitch *(as indicated by the black line)* to make the beads sit correctly and weave back to position yourself to add the accent bead.

6 Add the accent bead and weave back to position yourself for Step 2. Repeat Steps 2 to 6 until the desired length.

Squares Within

by Jill Oxton

Worked in square stitch.

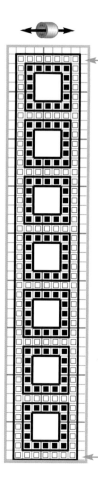

Thread up the first row of beads in the same direction as the arrow.

Similar in style to the Delica Bracelet on page 78, the accent beads are placed on in a different direction.

This bracelet is worked solely in square stitch.

Square Stitch instructions are on page 64 and additional instructions are on page 81.

Centre point for a 15.5cm length.

Quantity is for a 15.5 cm length

Miyuki Delica 11/0 Key		Qty
■ DBR 10	■ Black	224
□ DBR 331	▨ Gold	252
4mm Square 2006		15

Other Materials:

Nymo D - Black
2 x Gold Cover tips
1 x Gold Bracelet Clasp
2 x 3mm Gold Jump Rings
Clear Nail Polish

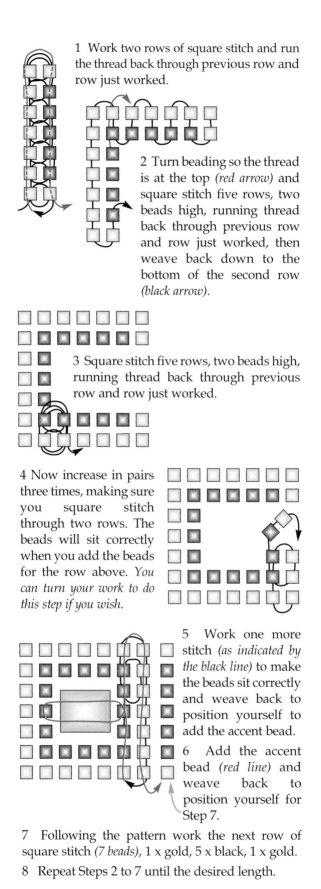

1 Work two rows of square stitch and run the thread back through previous row and row just worked.

2 Turn beading so the thread is at the top *(red arrow)* and square stitch five rows, two beads high, running thread back through previous row and row just worked, then weave back down to the bottom of the second row *(black arrow)*.

3 Square stitch five rows, two beads high, running thread back through previous row and row just worked.

4 Now increase in pairs three times, making sure you square stitch through two rows. The beads will sit correctly when you add the beads for the row above. *You can turn your work to do this step if you wish.*

5 Work one more stitch *(as indicated by the black line)* to make the beads sit correctly and weave back to position yourself to add the accent bead.

6 Add the accent bead *(red line)* and weave back to position yourself for Step 7.

7 Following the pattern work the next row of square stitch *(7 beads)*, 1 x gold, 5 x black, 1 x gold.

8 Repeat Steps 2 to 7 until the desired length.

Chunky

by Jill Oxton

Uses a combination of square stitch and ladder stitch

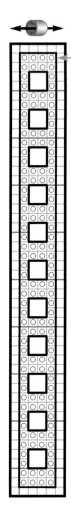

Thread up the first row of beads in the same direction as the arrow.

The chunky bracelet actually looks nicer when it is being worn, rather than laid out flat.

This chart is for a 16cm length worked using Miyuki 4mm Squares.

For a more delicate look use 3mm squares.

WE USED:

140 x Miyuki 4mm Squares - SQ290

11 x 6mm Diameter Round Red/Blue Glass Beads

OTHER MATERIALS:

Nymo D - Blue

2 x Cover tips

1 Bracelet Clasp

2 Jump Rings

Clear Nail Polish

Chunky Bracelet was worked in a combination of square stitch and ladder stitch, increasing and decreasing as indicated on the chart (see diagrams below). Work firmly and when each row is worked run the thread back through the previous row and then the row that was just worked (method 7c) to make the beading firmer and the beads sit nicely.

We used 4mm Delica Squares, Blue Nymo D thread and a John James 10 Tapestry Pointed Short Beading Needle.

1 Work two rows of square stitch *(black line)* and run back through the two rows *(red line)*.

2 Work two beads in ladder stitch *making several stitches so they are very firm* and then weave back through row 1.

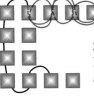

3 Work four beads in ladder stitch *making several stitches so they are very firm.*

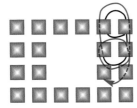

4 Pick up two beads and work a square stitch through the top row of beads. .
Repeat two more times.

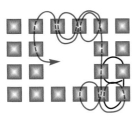

5 Work a square stitch through the last pair of beads added to make them sit properly and weave back to centre of square, reinforcing previous ladder stitch rows at the same time.

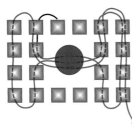

6 Pick up Accent Bead and place in centre of hole, going though the bead several times to secure it.

7 Repeat steps 2 to 6 until bracelet is the desired length.

Abacus

BY JILL OXTON

USES A COMBINATION OF SQUARE STITCH
AND LADDER STITCH

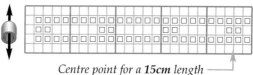

Centre point for a **15cm** length ⎯⎯⎯

For the Abacus I Bracelet above we used:

102 x Miyuki 4mm Square #2066 Green

90 x Mill Hill 11/0 Seed Bead 02053 Green

Green Nymo D thread.

Abacus I is worked in the same manner as the Chunky Bracelet on page 82, but we have an open space five beads wide. When the bracelet is complete, run thread back, threading up three 11/0 seed beads in each open space.

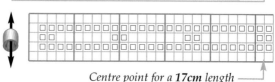

Centre point for a **17cm** length ⎯⎯⎯

For Abacus II above we used:

102 x Miyuki 4mm Square #401FR Purple/Blue

72 x Mill Hill 8/0 Seed Bead 18027 Caspian Blue

Black Nymo D thread.

Abacus II is worked in the same manner as the Chunky Bracelet on page 82, but we have an open space of six beads, *making a longer bracelet*. When the bracelet is complete, run thread back, threading up two 8/0 seed beads in each open space.

The Clasps *(also refer to pages 75 and 102).*

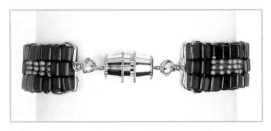

Above: We used a Barrel Clasp and this was attached to the bracelet by wire as I couldn't manage to slip a jump ring through the square.

We used 26 gauge non-tarnish wire 23 cm (9") long for each side. *I know this may seem excessive, but you will find it extremely fiddly if you use a shorter length.*

1   Cut wire 23cm (9") long and thread wire through the end row of beads, keeping equal lengths on both sides.

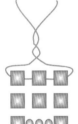

2   Tightly twist the ends together about three times, as close to the beads as you can without buckling them.

3   Place both ends together and make a loop, using a skewer or knitting needle as a form, and wrap the wire around the neck twice.

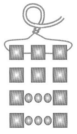

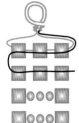

4   Run the ends of the wire back through the last two rows of the beads.

Repeat for other side.

Pull wire taut and cut with diagonal wire cutters.

If it is any consolation, I had about three go's at doing this before I did it satisfactorily.

Triangles & Crystals

by Jill Oxton

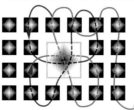

Thread up the first row of beads in the same direction as the arrow.

This bracelet was worked in the same manner as the Chunky Bracelet on page 82, except for the method used to stitch in the button (see diagram below) as it had four holes in the backing.

We used

260 x Miyuki 11/0 Triangles TR11 Black

21 x Maria George Crystal Buttons AB201

Black Nymo D

Centre point for a 16cm length.

Follow the instructions on page 83 from Steps 1 to 5.

6 Pick up Crystal Button and sew in centre hole, going though the button several times to secure it.

7 Repeat steps 2 to 6 until the bracelet is the desired length.

Scallops

You can obtain a delightful scalloped effect when you increase within the beading and step up and down with different sized seed beads.

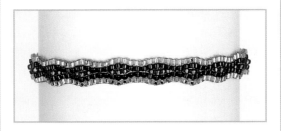

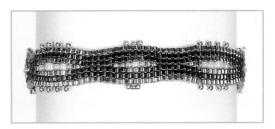

We have given charts and written instructions for these four designs. The shape is achieved by increasing within the design *(not on the edges)* and using graduated sizes of beads.

Scalloped Bracelet No. 1

BY JILL OXTON

DO NOT USE BLACK NYMO D AS IT IS TOO THICK FOR THE 15/0 SEED BEADS.

This bracelet was worked in square stitch and when each row was worked, the thread was run back through the previous row and then the row that was just worked to tighten up the beading and make the scallops stand out.

As you may initially find the chart a bit confusing, we have also written the pattern below.

Row 1: Thread up 4 x DBR42.

Rows 2 to 5: In square stitch work, 1 x DBR42, 2 x DBR507 and 1 x DBR42.

Row 6: Work 1 x DBR42, 1 x DBR507, *slip on 1 x 15/0,* work 1 x DBR507 *next to the third DBR in the previous row,* then 1 x DBR42.

Row 7: Work 1 x DBR42, 1 x DBR507, *work 1 x 11/0 Cream into the 15/0 that was slipped on in the previous row,* then 1 x DBR507 and 1 x DBR42.

Row 8: Work 1 x DBR42, 1 x DBR507, *now work 1 x 15/0 into the 11/0 Cream worked in previous row,* then 1 x DBR507 and 1 x DBR42.

Row 9: Work 1 x DBR42, 1 x DBR507, *miss the 15/0 that was worked in the previous row,* then 1 x DBR507 into the DBR507 of the previous row and 1 x DBR42.

Rows 10 to 12: Work, 1 x DBR42, 2 x DBR507 and 1 x DBR42.

Row 13: Repeat rows 6 to 12 until the bracelet is the desired length, then work one row of DBR42.

Upon completion of the bracelet, we pushed the increase beads out, so they are raised on one side and depressed on the other and placed a dab of nail polish into the depressions, to ensure they stayed that way.

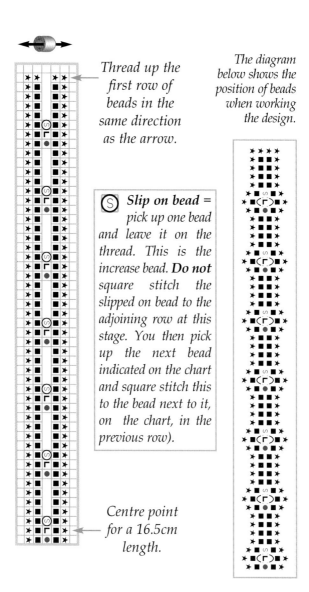

Thread up the first row of beads in the same direction as the arrow.

The diagram below shows the position of beads when working the design.

Ⓢ **Slip on bead =** *pick up one bead and leave it on the thread. This is the increase bead. **Do not** square stitch the slipped on bead to the adjoining row at this stage. You then pick up the next bead indicated on the chart and square stitch this to the bead next to it, on the chart, in the previous row).*

Centre point for a 16.5cm length.

COLOUR KEY			QTY
★ DBR 42		Gold	204
■ DBR 507		Gold/Purple Iris	196
Ⓢ MH 40123		Cream 15/0	28
L MH 00123		Cream 11/0	14
● MH 40123		Cream 15/0 DUPLICATED	

DBR = Miyuki Delica 11/0
MH = Mill Hill Seed Beads

OTHER MATERIALS:
Nymo D - Gold
2 x Gold Cover tips
1 x Gold Bracelet Clasp
2 x 3mm Gold Jump Rings
Clear Nail Polish

Scalloped Bracelet No. 2

(A variation on No. 1)

BY JILL OXTON

DO NOT USE BLACK NYMO D AS IT IS TOO THICK FOR THE 15/0 SEED BEADS.

This bracelet was worked in square stitch and when each row was worked, the thread was run back through the previous row and then the row that was just worked to tighten up the beading and make the scallops stand out.

As you may initially find the chart a bit confusing, we have also written the pattern below.

Row 1: Thread up 4 x DBR42.

Rows 2 TO 4: In square stitch work, 1 x DBR42, 2 x DBR10 and 1 x DBR42.

Row 5: Work 1 x DBR42, 1 x DBR10, *slip on 1 x 15/0,* work 1 x DBR10 *next to the third DBR10 in the previous row,* then 1 x DBR42.

Row 6: Work 1 x DBR42, 1 x DBR10, *work 1 x 11/0 Magenta into the 15/0 that was slipped on in the previous row,* then 1 x DBR10 and 1 x DBR42.

Row 7: Work 1 x DBR42, 1 x DBR10, *now work 1 x 15/0 into the 11/0 Magenta worked in previous row,* then 1 x DBR10 and 1 x DBR42.

Row 8: Work 1 x DBR42, 1 x DBR10, *miss the 15/0 that was worked in the previous row,* then 1 x DBR10 into the DBR10 of the previous row and 1 x DBR42.

Rows 9 & 10: Work, 1 x DBR42, 2 x DBR10 and 1 x DBR42.

Row 11: Repeat rows 5 to 10 until the bracelet is the desired length, then work one row of DBR42.

Upon completion of the bracelet, we pushed the increase beads out, so they are raised on one side and depressed on the other and placed a dab of nail polish into the depressions, to ensure they stayed that way.

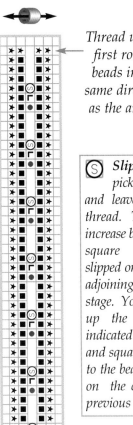

Thread up the
first row of
beads in the
same direction
as the arrow.

The diagram
below shows the
position of beads
when working
the design.

> Ⓢ **Slip on bead =**
> pick up one bead
> and leave it on the
> thread. This is the
> increase bead. **Do not**
> square stitch the
> slipped on bead to the
> adjoining row at this
> stage. You then pick
> up the next bead
> indicated on the chart
> and square stitch this
> to the bead next to it,
> on the chart, in the
> previous row).

Centre point
for a 16.5cm
length.

COLOUR KEY

				QTY
★	DBR 42		Gold	200
■	DBR 10		Gold/Purple Iris	192
Ⓢ	MH 42039		Green 15/0	32
L	MH 02077		Magenta 11/0	16
●	MH 42039		Green 15/0 DUPLICATED	

DBR = Miyuki Delica 11/0
MH = Mill Hill Seed Beads

OTHER MATERIALS:
Nymo D - Gold
2 x Gold Cover tips
1 x Gold Bracelet Clasp
2 x 3mm Gold Jump Rings
Clear Nail Polish

Scalloped

Bracelet with Picots

BY JILL OXTON

DO NOT USE BLACK NYMO D AS IT IS TOO THICK FOR THE 15/0 SEED BEADS.

This bracelet was worked in square stitch and when each row was worked, the thread was run back through the previous row and then the row that was just worked to tighten up the beading and make the scallops stand out.

THE PICOTS on the edge of the bracelet are added when running the thread back through the previous row and the row just worked.

As you may initially find the chart a bit confusing, we have also written the pattern on page 94.

TO FINISH OFF THE BRACELET and for a colour variation, see the instructions on page 96 and 97.

COLOUR KEY

				QTY
⌘	DBR42		Gold 11/0	286
+	Gold		*Gold Seed* **15/0**	12
■	DBR10		Black 11/0	298
S	Red		*Red Seed* **15/0***	12
II	Red		*Red Seed* **11/0***	13
M	Red		*Red Seed* **9/0***	6
L	Red		*Red Seed* **8/0***	3

We used graduating sizes of Silver-Lined Red Beads of a similar colour, but used Miyuki Delica 11/0 for the border and background.

*You could also use 15/0, 11/0, 10/0 and 9/0 if you have them.

OTHER MATERIALS:
Nymo D - Gold
2 x Gold Cover tips
1 x Gold Bracelet Clasp
2 x 3mm Gold Jump Rings
Clear Nail Polish

Bracelet pictured at actual size.

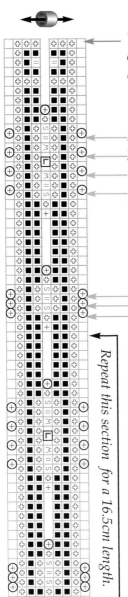

Thread up the first row of beads in the same direction as the arrow.

Add pairs of picots after this row has been worked and when you are running the thread back through the previous row and the row just worked.

Repeat this section for a 16.5cm length.

CHART EXPLANATIONS - *See diagram below*

Ignore the blank areas on the chart, *these allow space on the chart for the increases within.*

⊕ **Slip on bead =** pick up one bead and leave it on the thread, *do not* square stitch it to the adjoining row at this stage, then you will need to pick up the next bead, *as indicated on the chart.*

Where the **L** symbol appears on the chart, work the first row as charted and include the **L** - 8/0 bead, then work the second row as charted and pass the thread through the 8/0 bead.

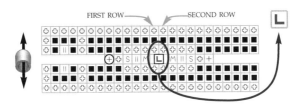

FIRST ROW SECOND ROW L

Scalloped Bracelet with Picots
as charted on page 93.

*After each row is square stitched, run thread back through all of the beads of the previous row and then the row just worked. The **15/0 gold picots** on the edge of the bracelet are added when doing this.*

Row 1: String up, 6 x DBR42.

Row 2: 1 x DBR42, 4 x DBR10 and 1 x DBR42.

Row 3: 1 x DBR42, 1 x DBR10, **2 x Red 11/0,** 1 x DBR10 and   1 x DBR42.

Row 4: 1 x DBR42, 4 x DBR10 and 1 x DBR42.

Row 5: 6 x DBR42.

Row 6 & 7: 1 x DBR42, 4 x DBR10 and 1 x DBR42.

Row 8 Increase Row: 1 x DBR42, 2 x DBR10, *slip on 1 x 15/0 gold,* 2 x DBR10 and 1 x DBR42.

Row 9: 1 x DBR42, 2 x DBR10, 1 x DBR42 *next to 15/0 slip on bead of previous row,* 2 x DBR10 and 1 x DBR42.

Row 10: 1 x DBR42, 1 x DBR10, 1 x DBR42, **1 x 15/0 Red**, 1 x DBR42, 1 x DBR10 and 1 x DBR42.

Row 11: 1 x DBR42, 1 x DBR10, 1 x DBR42, **1 x 11/0 Red**, 1 x DBR42, 1 x DBR10 and 1 x DBR42. *Work picot on each edge when running thread back through the previous row and the row just worked.*

Row 12: 1 x DBR42, 1 x DBR10, 1 x DBR42, **1 x 9/0 Red**, 1 x DBR42, 1 x DBR10 and 1 x DBR42.

Row 13: 1 x DBR42, 1 x DBR10, 1 x DBR42, **1 x 8/0 Red**, 1 x DBR42, 1 x DBR10 and 1 x DBR42. *Work picot on each edge when running thread back through the previous row and the row just worked.*

Row 14: 1 x DBR42, 1 x DBR10, 1 x DBR42, *slip thread through 8/0 Red of previous row*, 1 x DBR42, 1 x DBR10 and 1 x DBR42.

Row 15: 1 x DBR42, 1 x DBR10, 1 x DBR42, **1 x 9/0 Red**, 1 x DBR42, 1 x DBR10 and 1 x DBR42. *Work picot on each edge when running thread back through the previous row and the row just worked.*

Row 16: 1 x DBR42, 1 x DBR10, 1 x DBR42, **1 x 11/0 Red**, 1 x DBR42, 1 x DBR10 and 1 x DBR42.

Row 17: 1 x DBR42, 1 x DBR10, 1 x DBR42, **1 x 15/0 Red**, 1 x DBR42, 1 x DBR10 and 1 x DBR42. *Work picot on each edge when running thread back through the previous row and the row just worked.*

ROW 18: 1 x DBR42, 2 x DBR10, 1 x DBR42 *next to 15/0 Red,* 2 x DBR10 and 1 x DBR42.

ROW 19: 1 x DBR42, 2 x DBR10, *1 x 15/0 gold,* 2 x DBR10 and 1 x DBR42.

ROW 20 DECREASE ROW: 1 x DBR42, 2 x DBR10, miss the *15/0 gold of previous row,* 2 x DBR10 and 1 x DBR42.

ROWS 21 TO 24: 1 x DBR42, 4 x DBR10 and 1 x DBR42.

ROW 25 INCREASE ROW: 1 x DBR42, 2 x DBR10, *slip on 1 x 15/0 gold,* 2 x DBR10 and 1 x DBR42.

ROW 26: 1 x DBR42, 2 x DBR10, 1 x DBR42 *next to 15/0 slip on bead of previous row,* 2 x DBR10 and 1 x DBR42.

ROW 27: 1 x DBR42, 1 x DBR10, 1 x DBR42, **1 x 15/0 Red,** 1 x DBR42, 1 x DBR10 and 1 x DBR42.

ROW 28: 1 x DBR42, 1 x DBR10, 1 x DBR42, **1 x 11/0 Red,** 1 x DBR42, 1 x DBR10 and 1 x DBR42. *Work picot on each edge when running thread back through the previous row and the row just worked.*

ROW 29: 1 x DBR42, 1 x DBR10, 1 x DBR42, **1 x 15/0 Red,** 1 x DBR42, 1 x DBR10 and 1 x DBR42. *Work picot on each edge when running thread back through the previous row and the row just worked.*

ROW 30: 1 x DBR42, 2 x DBR10, 1 x DBR42 *next to 15/0 Red,* 2 x DBR10 and 1 x DBR42. *Work picot on each edge when running thread back through the previous row and the row just worked.*

ROW 31: 1 x DBR42, 2 x DBR10, *1 x 15/0 gold,* 2 x DBR10 and 1 x DBR42.

continued on page 96

Row 32 Decrease Row: 1 x DBR42, 2 x DBR10, miss the *15/0 gold bead of previous row*, 2 x DBR10 and 1 x DBR42.

Rows 33 to 36: 1 x DBR42, 4 x DBR10 and 1 x DBR42.

Rows 37 to 65: Repeat rows 8 to 36.

Rows 66 to 91: Repeat rows 8 to 33 once more for a 16m length.

End the bracelet by working

Row 92: 6 x DBR42.

Row 93: 1 x DBR42, 4 x DBR10 and 1 x DBR42.

Row 94: 1 x DBR42, 1 x DBR10, 2 x **Red 11/0,** 1 x DBR10 and 1 x DBR42.

Row 95: 1 x DBR42, 4 x DBR10 and 1 x DBR42.

Row 96: 6 x DBR42.

Weave in the thread ends and attach bracelet findings using a new piece of thread.

We used a 15/0 gold seed bead between the bracelet and the cover tip. I thought that this made the cover tip sit much nicer!

Finishing Off The Bracelet

To ensure the accent beads in the centre of the bracelet stood proud, *as some of them tend to slip back behind the other beads,* we painted these sections on the back of the bracelet with a coat of nail polish. *(I really like to use Sally Hansen's Double Duty Clear Top Coat).*

We let this "touch" dry and then pushed the centre (red) beads out to the right side of the bracelet.

When they were all sitting nicely, we painted another thicker coat of nail varnish onto these sections on the back and let it harden overnight.

Pearl Version
of Scalloped Bracelet
with Picots

The Pearl & Gold Bracelet *pictured left is a colour variation using different sized beads and Delica's.*

Colour Key			Qty
✛ DBR34		Gold 11/0	286
+ Gold		*Seed* **15/0**	12
■ DBR23		Bronze Iris	298
S Cream		*Seed* **15/0**	12
‖ Cream		*Seed* **11/0**	13
M Cream		*Seed* **11/0***	6
L Cream		*Seed* **8/0**	3

We used Cream Nymo D.

*I could only find three sizes in the cream/pearl bead that matched in my bead stash. You can also use sizes 15/0, 11/0, 10/0, 9/0 or 8/0, as long as the beads graduate in size.

When choosing your own colours for this bracelet, make sure that the background colour is quite dark or the gold border and edgings around the accent beads will not stand out.

Pearl Scallop Bracelet pictured left at actual size.

Wire Knit Bracelet

BY BEVERLEY WELLS

MATERIALS

1 Packet Mill Hill 6/0 Glass Beads

9 each of Nine Different types and shapes of embellishment beads. *Our model used 5/0, 6/0, 7/0 and 8/0 rounds, squares, ovals and discs.*

1 x Bracelet Clasp

2 x 3 Hole Bar Ends

2 x 5mm Jump Rings

1 x Reel 28 gauge Coloured Wire

1 x Pair of 3mm Knitting Needles

METHOD:

STEP 1: Separate each different shape and type of bead into their own group, so you have nine piles of beads, plus the Mill Hill 6/0's.

THESE NINE BEAD GROUPS ARE REFERRED TO AS L.

THE MILL HILL 6/0 BEADS ARE REFERRED TO AS S.

STEP 2: Unwind *(do not cut)* 30cm of wire.

Picking up a **different L** each time, thread the beads onto the wire in the following order.

(1L, 1S) 3 times, (1S, 1L) 3 times.

Repeat from * to * until all of the embellishment beads have been threaded onto the wire. Finishing at the end of a complete set or combination of beads.

Let the weight of the beads unravel the wire, instead of pulling the wire off the reel, as this helps to prevent tangles and kinks in the wire.

Row1: Leaving a 30cm tail, *(this is used to sew the bar end onto your knitting)* cast on 5 stitches and knit one row without beads.

Row 2: With the working needle in the knit position *slide one bead up to the needle and knit the stitch*. Repeat from * to * four more times.

Row 3: *This and then every alternate row has only one bead added, which is used on the first stitch.*

With the needle in the knit position, slide up one bead and then knit across the five stitches without sliding on any more beads.

Repeat rows 2 and 3 until the bracelet is the desired length, less the bar ends, jump rings and the clasp.

To End: Knit one row without beads and cast off, leaving a 30cm tail before cutting the wire.

Using the wire tail, attach a 3 hole bar to each end of the bracelet, weaving the excess wire securely into the bracelet.

Attach the bracelet clasp to the 3 hole bar using the jump rings.

Gallery

Above: The blue bracelet above was made by threading elastic through the large oval bead and using smaller beads as spacers.

The elastic was knotted and the knot was hidden inside one of the large beads.

Below: The wire cuff was made using wire that Jo found in her shed. Threading beads onto the wire and twisting the wire into a pleasing shape.

A nice feature is the spiral hinge that Jo added in the front of the bracelet.

BRACELETS BY **JO GARDNER**

BEAD TIPS

also known as fold over cover tips, bead tips, clam shell tips or Charlotte crimps.

The bead tip acts as a transition between the beading thread and metal findings. Using it, rather than stitching your finding onto beaded jewellery, will finish the piece off and make it look more professional.

Attaching a cover tip to an even number of beads.

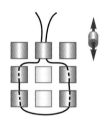

Attaching a cover tip to an odd number of beads.

TO ATTACH A BEAD TIP
(See the diagrams on right.)

Pass the thread through the bead tip (there is a hole at the base). Run it through at least two rows of the beading if possible *(to make the end of the bracelet more stable)* and then bring the thread back out through the hole in the cover tip.

Thread a bead onto one of the threads (this stops the knot from falling through the hole) and tie two or three knots.

Attaching a cover tip to an odd number of beads.

Secure the knot with a dab of glue (or clear nail polish - this dries quicker, and comes with its own brush).

Using a pair of long nosed pliers, gently squeeze the bead tip closed over the bead, then bend the metal arm down over the cap to form a loop.

Place a jump ring or slip ring in the loop, and attach your other findings.

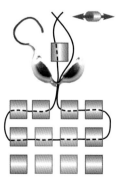

Attaching a cover tip to an even number of beads.

Findings

JUMP RINGS are split circles of wire used for connecting the metal findings together. Bend the jump ring sideways rather than opening it out, otherwise it will lose its shape. We mainly use 3mm and 5mm jump rings on most items.

SPRING-RING CLASPS are available in a range of sizes. Pictured left with ring and tag.

STERLING SILVER AND 9K GOLD FINDINGS ARE ALSO AVAILABLE FOR SPECIAL PIECES.

BARREL CLASPS can be awkward to close on a bracelet singlehanded.

PARROT/LOBSTER CLASPS & RING are easy to close.

RING & TOGGLE are my favourite closure and there are many different styles and sizes.

SPECTACLE HOLDERS are now available in black, clear and white in many pretty styles.

SHEPHERD HOOKS, studs and clip-on ear-ring findings are easy to find and inexpensive.

BEAD TIPS also known as fold over cover tips, bead tips, clam shell tips or Charlotte crimps.

Helpful Hints

Bead tips are made of base metal which cracks and breaks easily if bent too much. You safely only have one go at rounding off the hook and closing the bead tip, so don't fiddle around too much with them.

Bearing this in mind, I always use a new length of thread to attach my bead tips and findings in case they break or, because once they are attached I don't like them or have found something better.

It is so much easier to cut them off than try to achieve the impossible and unpick the thread, and possibly have to repair and reinforce beading.

If your beads are packed with thread, use a finer needle to attach the finding.

Bead tip →
Jump ring
15/0 seed bead

I recently found that a nice transition between the beading and the bead tip is to use 1 x 15/0 gold or silver seed bead between the bracelet and the bead tip. This seems to make the bead tip sit nicer and hides the thread that sometimes shows at the base of the bead tip.

3mm or 5mm diameter jump rings can be used to attach the bead tip to the bracelet clasp, but 3mm does look daintier.

Attaching a flower bead and leaf to the bracelet clasp also adds a nice touch.

These have been threaded onto a jump ring and attached to the ring of a ring and toggle.

Presentation can be everything. Pictured above is the Rose Bracelet from *Jill Oxton's Cross Stitch & Beading Issue 53*. This has been placed in a gift box that we purchased from our local jewellers.

WHEN USING A RING AND TOGGLE STYLE OF CLASP, you will need to make your bracelet a little shorter as you need either jump rings or an extra two or three beads threaded up on the end of the bracelet to make it easier to do up and undo. This is very important on a wide bracelet - *and a good reason to use fresh thread for attaching findings* - so it can be cut off easily if it doesn't work.